50 words about

Animals

David and Patricia Armentrout

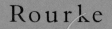

Rourke

Publishing LLC

Vero Beach, Florida 32964

www.rourkepublishing.com

PHOTO CREDITS: ©James P. Rowan page 28 bottom; © PhotoDisc all other photos

Editor: Frank Sloan

Cover and page design by Nicola Stratford

Library of Congress Cataloging-in-Publication Data

Armentrout, David, 1962-
 Animals / David and Patricia Armentrout.
    p. cm. — (50 words about)
Summary: Provides simple definitions for fifty words related to animals
along with sample sentences using each word.
 ISBN 1-58952-341-5 (hardcover)
 1. Animals—Juvenile literature. [1. Animals—Dictionaries.] I.
Armentrout, Patricia, 1960- II. Title.
 QL49 .A73 2002
 590—dc21   2002002364

Printed in the USA

CG/CG

animal (AN e mel)

Any living creature that can breathe and move about.

amphibian

A cold-blooded animal with a backbone which begins life in water and later lives on land.

An amphibian begins life with gills and later grows lungs.

antlers

Large, bony structures that grow from the heads of deer, elk, and moose.

Deer shed and grow new antlers each year.

baby

A very young animal.

A baby lion is called a lion cub.

beak

A hard, pointed outer part of the mouth.

The toucan is a tropical bird with a very large beak.

bird

A warm-blooded animal with wings, feathers, two legs, and a beak.

The penguin is a bird that does not fly.

camouflage

A color or cover that makes an animal look like its surroundings.

A white rabbit uses camouflage to hide in the snow.

carnivore

An animal that eats meat.

This carnivore is the largest member of the cat family.

claws

Hard, curved nails on the feet of some animals.

A colorful macaw uses its claws to grip its perch.

cold-blooded

Animals with body temperatures that stay about the same as their surroundings.

Alligators are cold-blooded and must sit in the sun to warm their bodies.

crustacean

A sea animal with a bony skeleton on the outside.

A crustacean depends on its outer shell for protection.

domestic

Animals that are no longer wild.

Sheep and other farm-raised animals are domestic animals.

eggs

Undeveloped young that have hard, protective shells.

Ducklings will soon hatch from these eggs.

endangered species

An animal in danger of disappearing forever.

The giant panda is an endangered species.

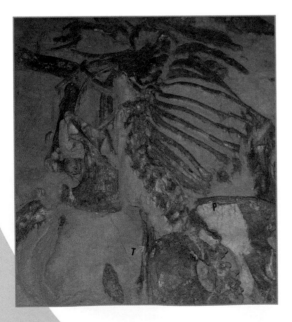

extinct

When an animal no longer lives or has died out.

This fossilized skeleton is from the extinct mammoth.

feathers

Light, fluffy parts that cover a bird's body.

A spoonbill pelican has pretty pink feathers.

female

The sex of an animal that gives birth or lays eggs.

Female cattle, called cows, produce milk for their young.

fish

A cold-blooded animal that lives in water.

Yellowtail snapper are saltwater fish.

fur

An animal's thick cover of fine hair.

A polar bear's fur provides warmth in cold Arctic waters.

habitat

The place where an animal lives.

An animal's habitat depends on the creature's need for food and water.

hair

Thin soft strands that grow on an animal's head or body.

A gorilla's body is covered in fine hair.

herbivore

An animal that eats only plants.

Rabbits belong to the herbivore group.

herd

A large group of animals.

It is possible to see a herd of buffalo in South Dakota.

hibernate

To spend the cold months inactive or in a deep sleep.

A grizzly bear mother and cub will hibernate through the winter.

horn

A hard, bony growth on the heads of some animals.

Horns grow larger over time and are not shed like antlers.

hunt

To search for food.

In order to survive, a cheetah must hunt for food.

insect

A small animal with six legs, three main body parts, and an outer skeleton.

A butterfly is an insect that feeds on the nectar of flowers.

invertebrate

An animal with no backbone.

Some invertebrates live on land while others, such as this striped shrimp, live in the sea.

male

The sex of an animal that can father young.

A male lion grows a mane of hair around its head.

mammal

A warm-blooded animal with a backbone.

A fox is a mammal that hunts rodents and eats wild fruit.

marsupial

An animal that carries its young in a belly pouch.

A famous Australian marsupial is the kangaroo.

migrate

To travel to another place the same time every year.

Humpback whales migrate to breed and feed.

nest

A place built by animals to lay eggs or to bring up their young.

A large bird of prey like the eagle builds a strong nest.

omnivore

An animal that eats both plants and meat.

Raccoons belong to the omnivore family and will eat many things including fish, berries, and nuts.

predator

An animal that hunts other animals for food.

The lion is a fierce predator.

prey

An animal that is hunted by another animal for food.

A chipmunk is prey to large birds such as hawks and eagles.

primate

A group of mammals including humans, apes, and monkeys.

An orangutan is a large, strong, and very smart primate.

reptile

A cold-blooded animal with a backbone and scaly skin.

A reptile can be found on land or in water.

scales

Small, hard plates that cover the bodies of some animals.

A chameleon's body is covered with hundreds of scales.

school

A group of fish or other sea creatures.

Some fish swim in a school to help protect themselves from predators.

sense

A power an animal uses to learn about its surroundings.

A snake uses its tongue as a powerful sense organ.

skeleton

The framework of bones in an animal's body.

A frog skeleton is very different from a human skeleton.

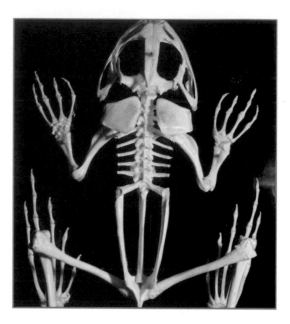

skin

The tough outside layer on an animal's body.

Walruses have tough skin that covers a thick layer of fat.

species

One certain kind of animal.

The bottlenose dolphin is one species of dolphin.

spider

A small animal with two body parts, eight legs, and no wings.

Some spiders spin a web to catch flies and other insects.

talons

Sharp claws of a bird.

An eagle uses its talons to grasp its prey.

teeth

Bony parts of the mouth used for biting and chewing.

Hippos use their teeth to chew water plants.

vertebrate

An animal with a backbone.

Vertebrates include fish, reptiles, birds, and mammals.

warm-blooded

Animals whose bodies always keep a warm, steady temperature.

Mammals are warm-blooded animals.

wild

An animal that lives without help from people.

Wild wolves live in family groups called packs.

zoology

The scientific study of animals.

Children who love animals sometimes grow up to study zoology.

Pronunciation Key

amphibian (am FIB ee en)
antlers (ANT lerz)
baby (BAY bee)
beak (BEEK)
bird (BERD)
camouflage (KAM uh flahzh)
carnivore (KAR nuh vor)
claws (KLAWZ)
cold-blooded
  (KOHLD BLUHD id)
crustacean (kruhs TAY shen)
domestic (duh MES tik)
eggs (EGZ)
endangered species
  (en DAYN jerd SPEE sheez)
extinct (ek STINGKT)
feathers (FETH erz)
female (FEE mayl)
fish (FISH)
fur (FER)
habitat (HAB uh tat)
hair (HAYR)
herbivore (ER be vor)
herd (HERD)
hibernate (HY ber nayt)
horn (HORN)
hunt (HUNT)
insect (IN sekt)

invertebrate
  (in VERT e bret)
male (MAYL)
mammal (MAM uhl)
marsupial
  (mar SOO pee uhl)
migrate (MY grayt)
nest (NEST)
omnivore (OM nuh vo)
predator (PRED uh te)
prey (PRAY)
primate (PRY mayt)
reptile (REP tyle)
scales (SKAYLZ)
school (SKOOL)
sense (SENS)
skeleton (SKEL uh tuhn)
skin (SKIN)
species (SPEE sheez)
spider (SPY der)
talons (TAL uhnz)
teeth (TEETH)
vertebrate (VER tuh bret)
warm-blooded
  (WORM BLUHD id)
wild (WYLD)
zoology
  (zoo ALL uh jee)

Did you know...

... all peacocks are male? Females are called peahens. Females don't have the beautiful tail feathers like the males.

Did you know...

...most starfish can regrow body parts? An arm broken off from one starfish can grow more arms and become a new starfish.

Did you know...

..a camel can survive several days without a drink of water? However, a thirsty camel can drink as much as 30 gallons (113.5 liters) of water at one time.

Did you know...

...a zebra's stripes can actually help them hide from predators? A lion has a hard time picking out just one zebra when they stand close together.

Did you know...

...the bat is not a bird? A bat is a winged mammal that can fly.

Did you know...

...the giraffe is the tallest of all animals? A giraffe can grow to 18 feet (5.49 meters).

Index

Further Reading

Taylor, Barbara. *Oxford First Book of Animals.*
Oxford University Press, 2000.

Taylor, Barbara and Steve Pollock. *Animal Kingdom.*
Silver Dolphin Press, 2000.

Websites to Visit

www.enchantedlearning.com

www.pbs.org

www.nationalgeographic.org

About the Authors

David and Patricia Armentrout specialize in nonfiction writing. They have had several books published for primary school reading. They reside in Cincinnati, Ohio, with their two children.